AF261519

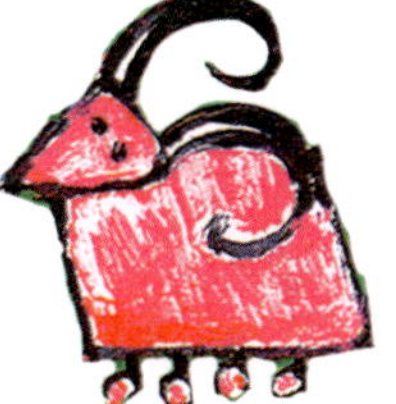

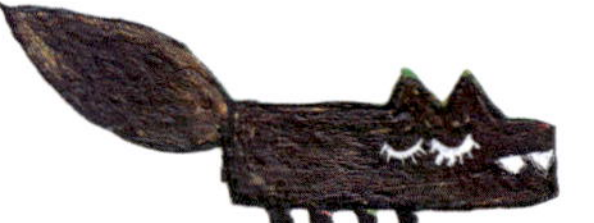
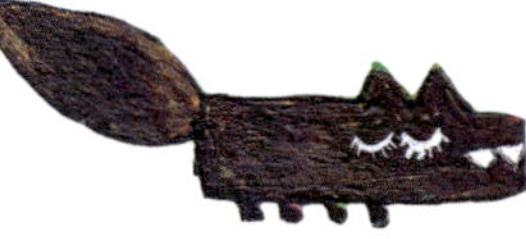
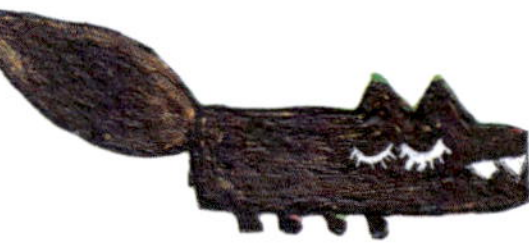
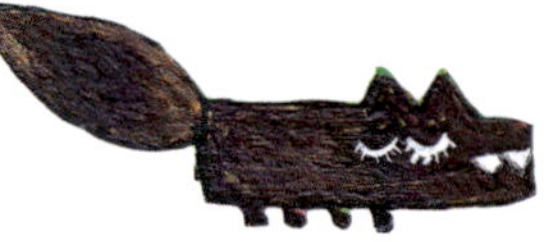

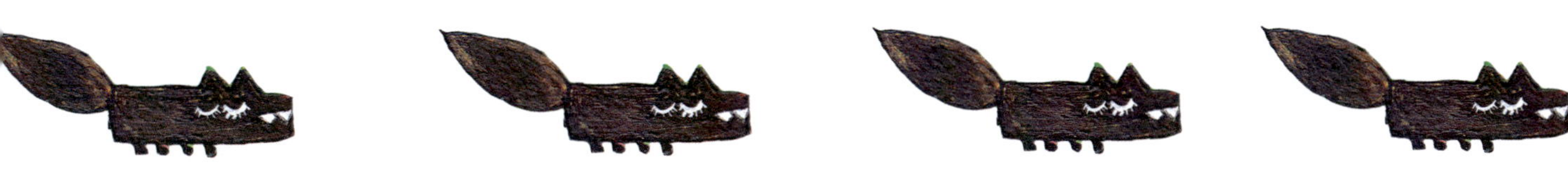

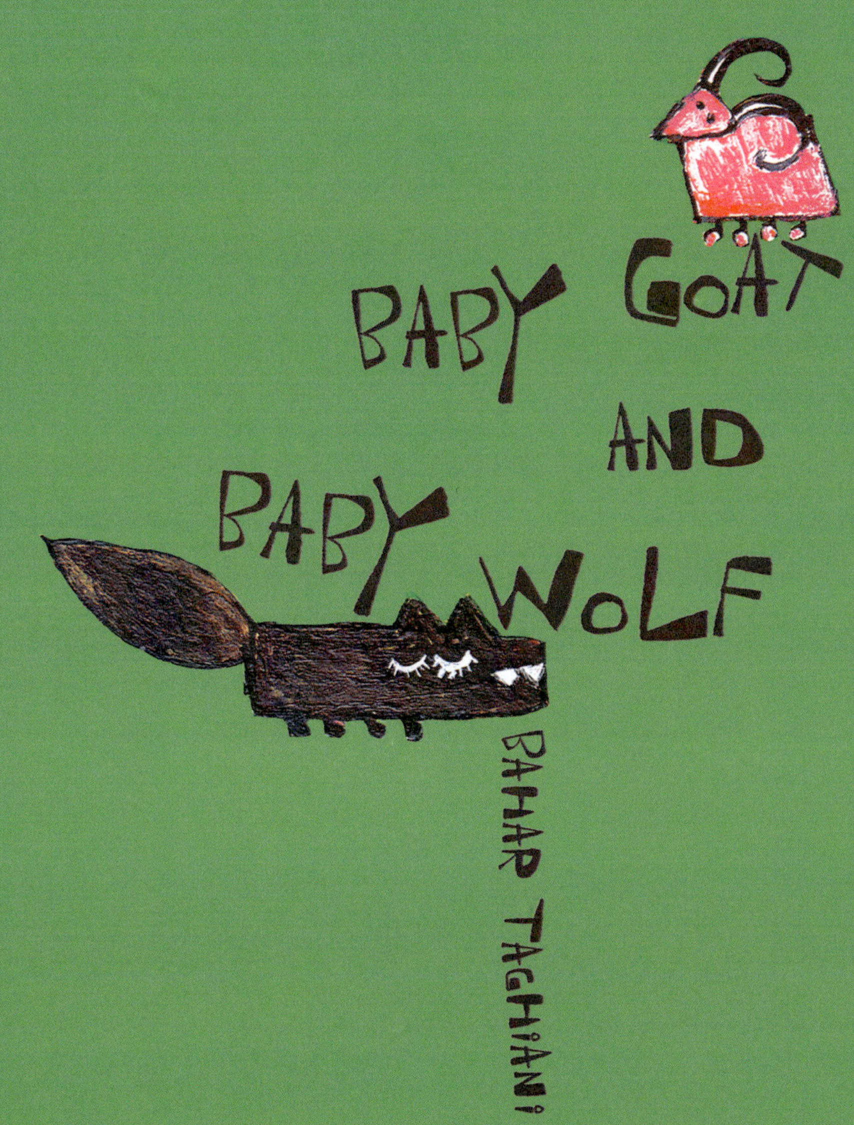

BABY GOAT AND BABY WOLF
BAHAR TAGHIANI

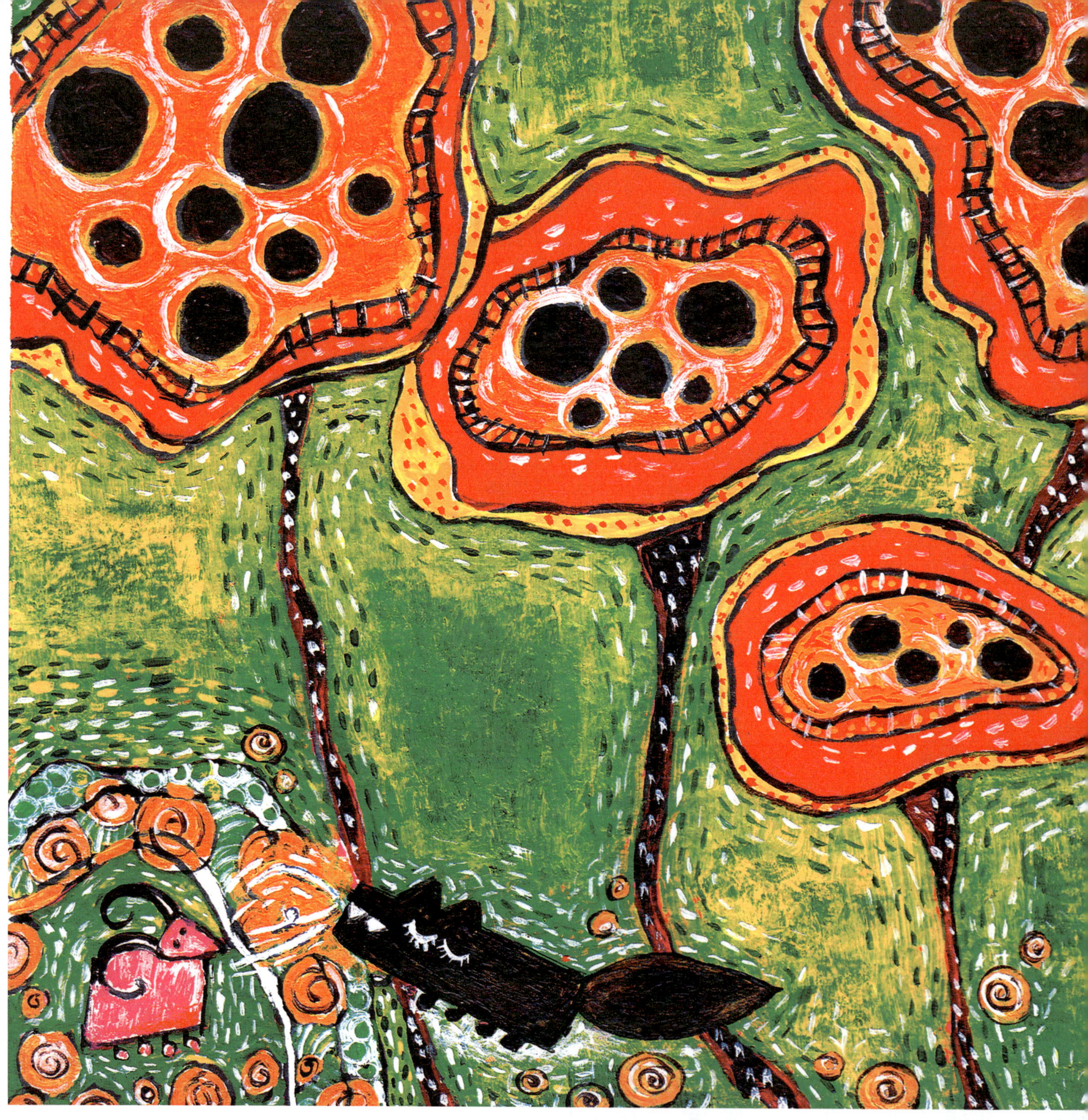

THE
BABY WOLF
IS SINGING.

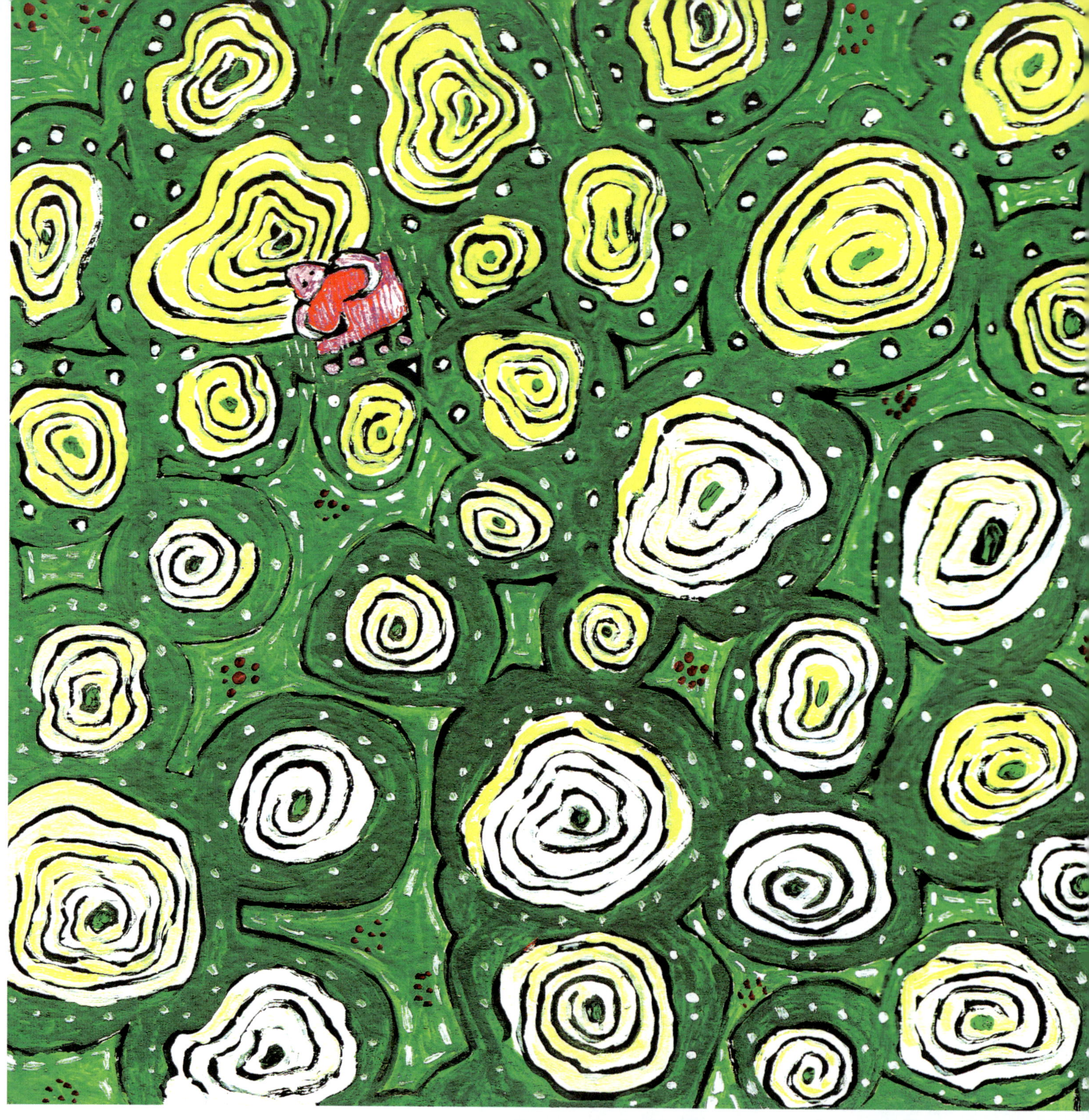

THE BABY GOAT IS EATING CABBAGE.

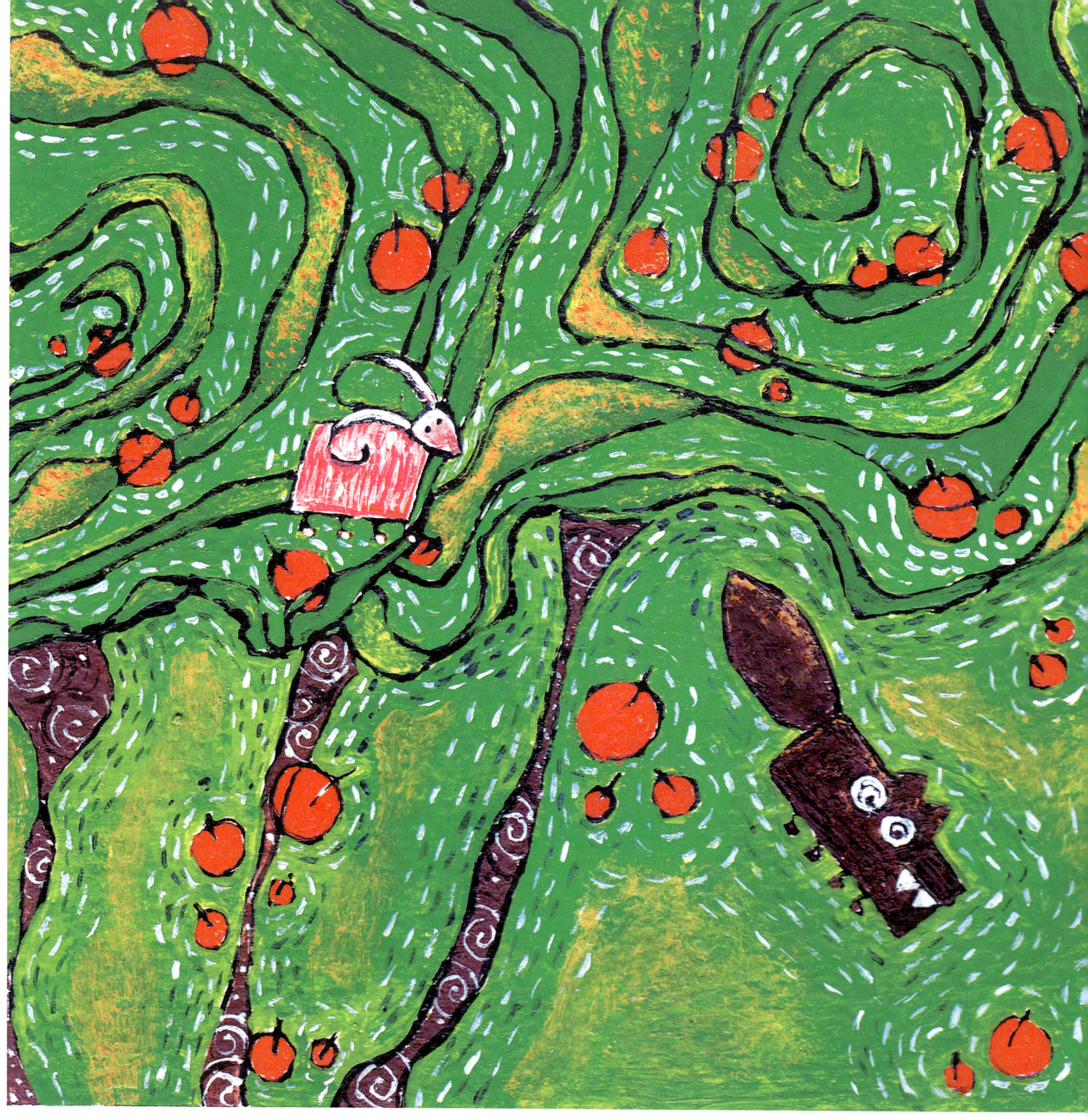

THE BABY GOAT
AND
THE BABY WOLF
ARE PICKING APPLES
TOGETHER...

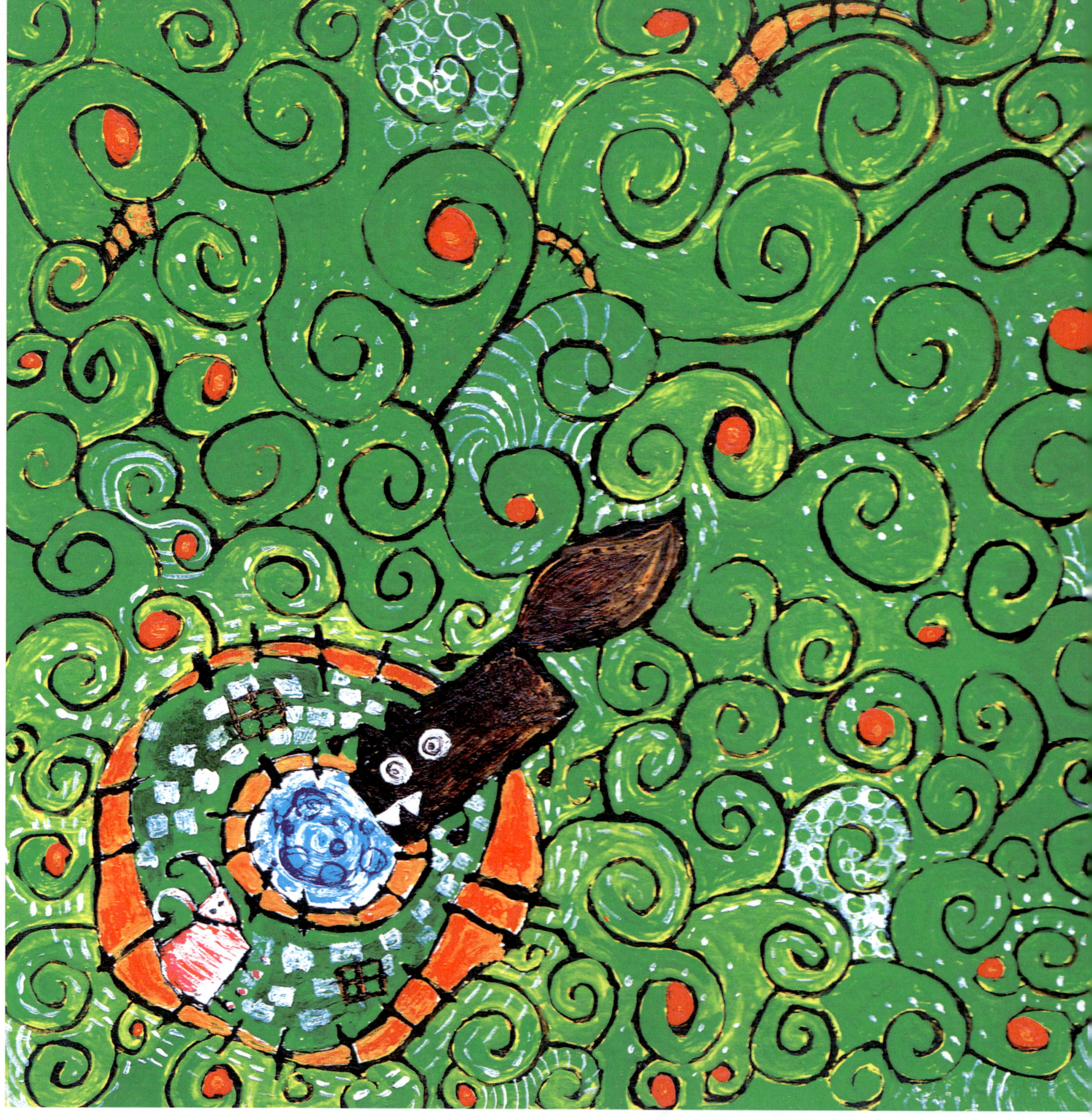

THE BABY GOAT
AND
THE BABY WOLF
ARE   PLAYING   IN
THE   WATER.

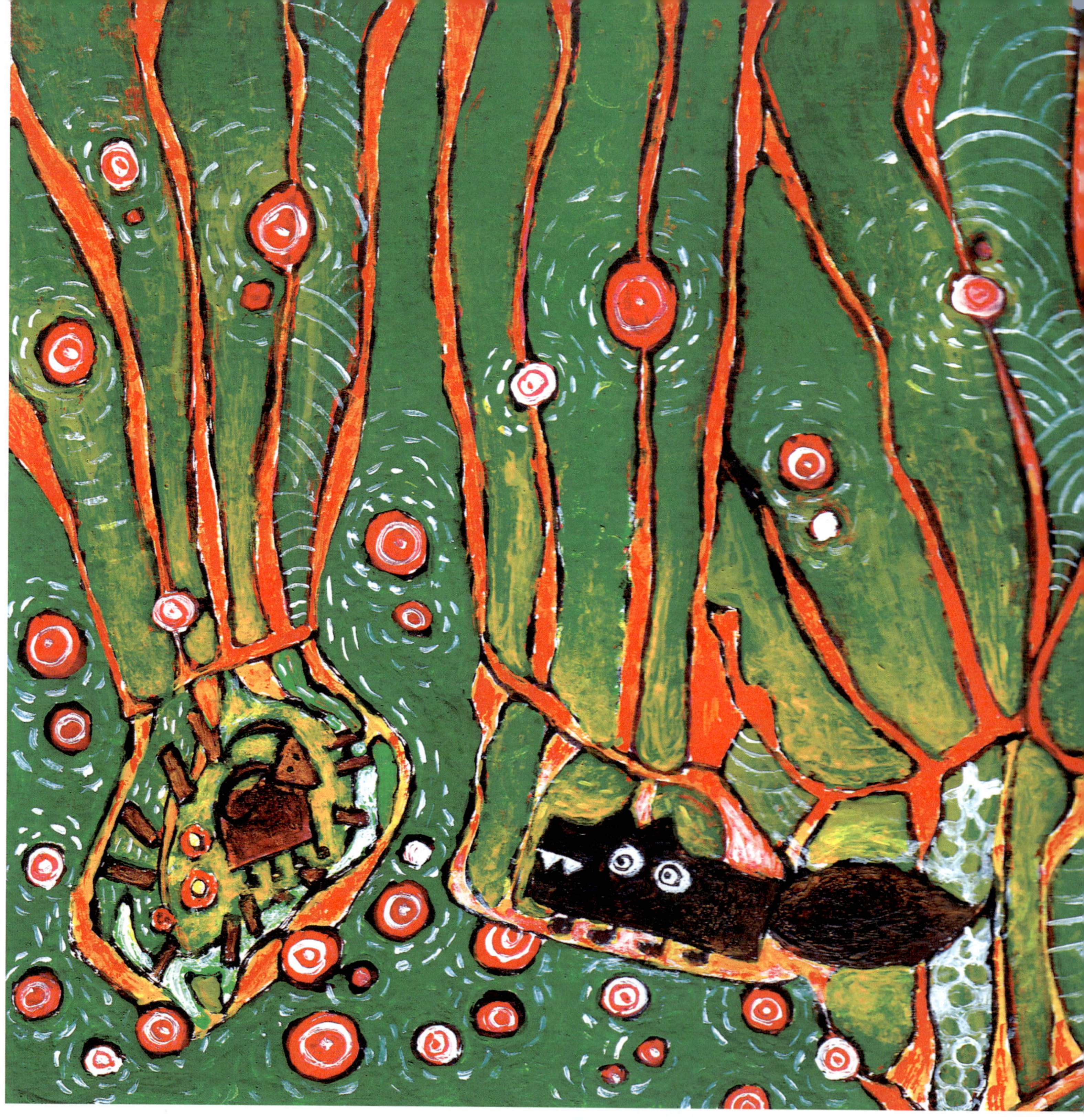

"ARE YOU LOST?"
THE DADDY GOAT
ASKS THE BABY WOLF.

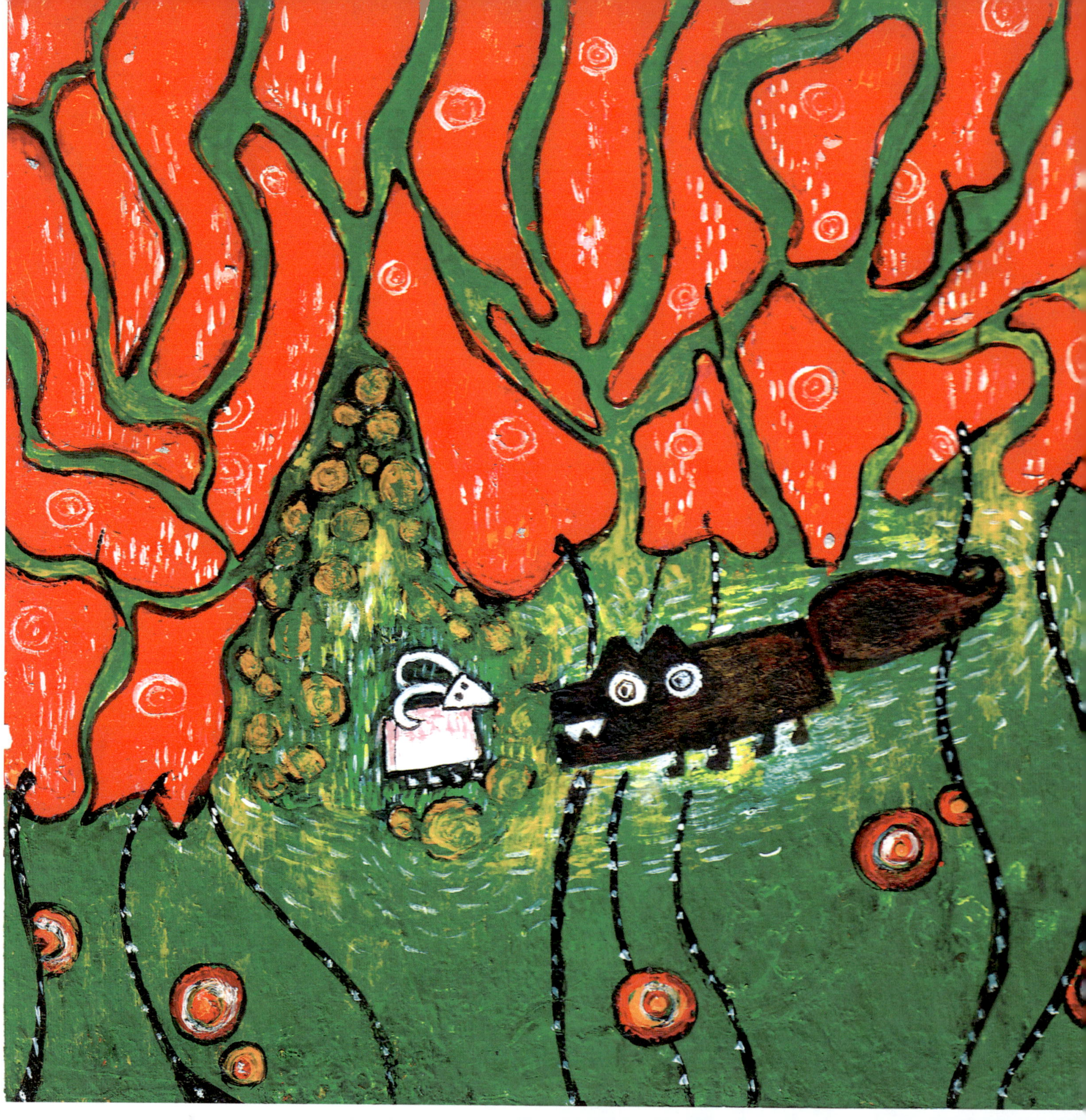

"WHO ARE YOU?"

THE MUMMY GOAT ASKS THE BABY WOLF.

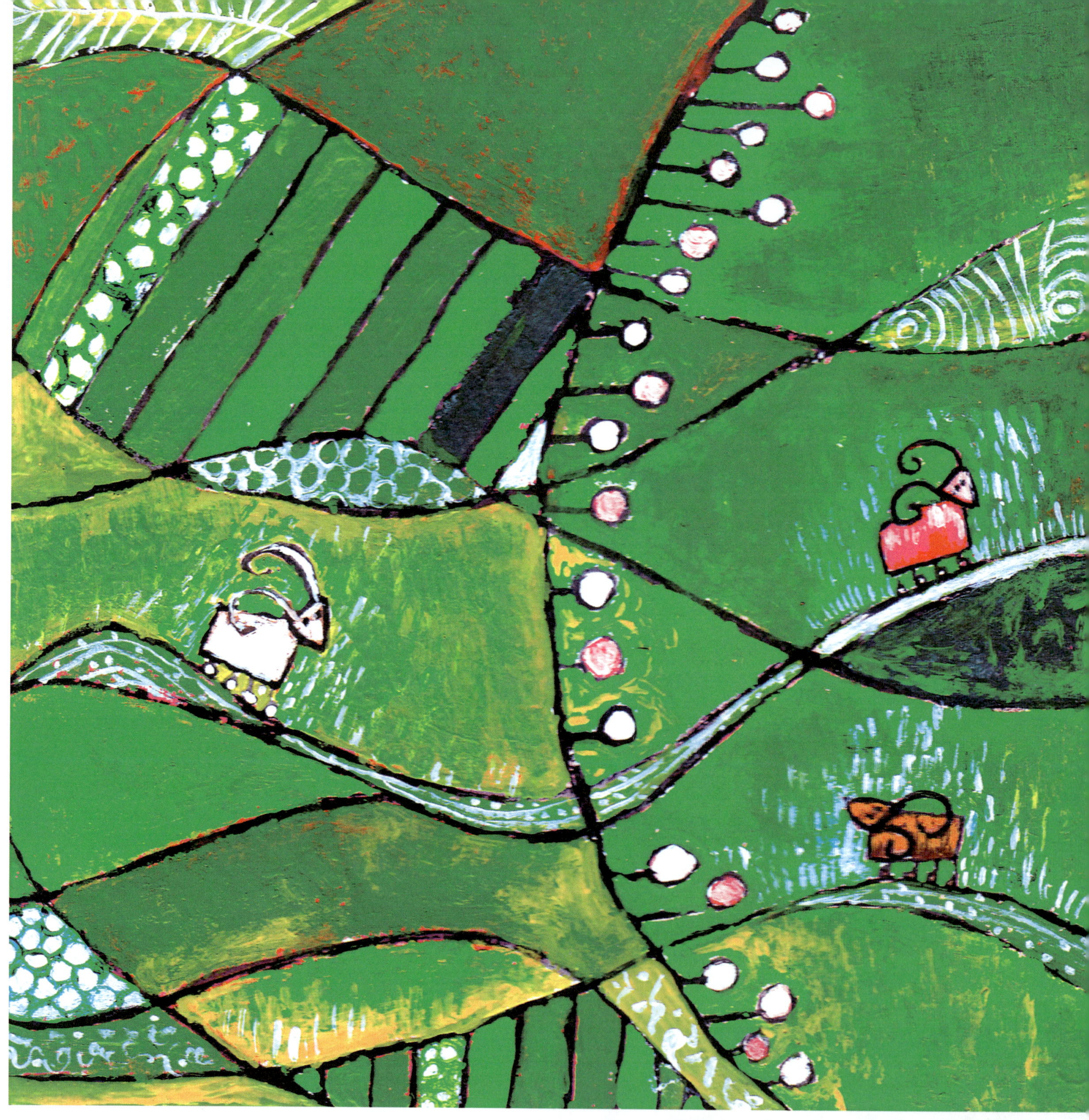

THE MUMMY GOAT AND THE DADDY GOAT FEEL A LITTLE WORRIED ABOUT THEIR BABY GOAT'S NEW FRIND, THE WOLF.

WHAT DO YOU THINK THEY SHOULD SAY TO THEIR CHILD?

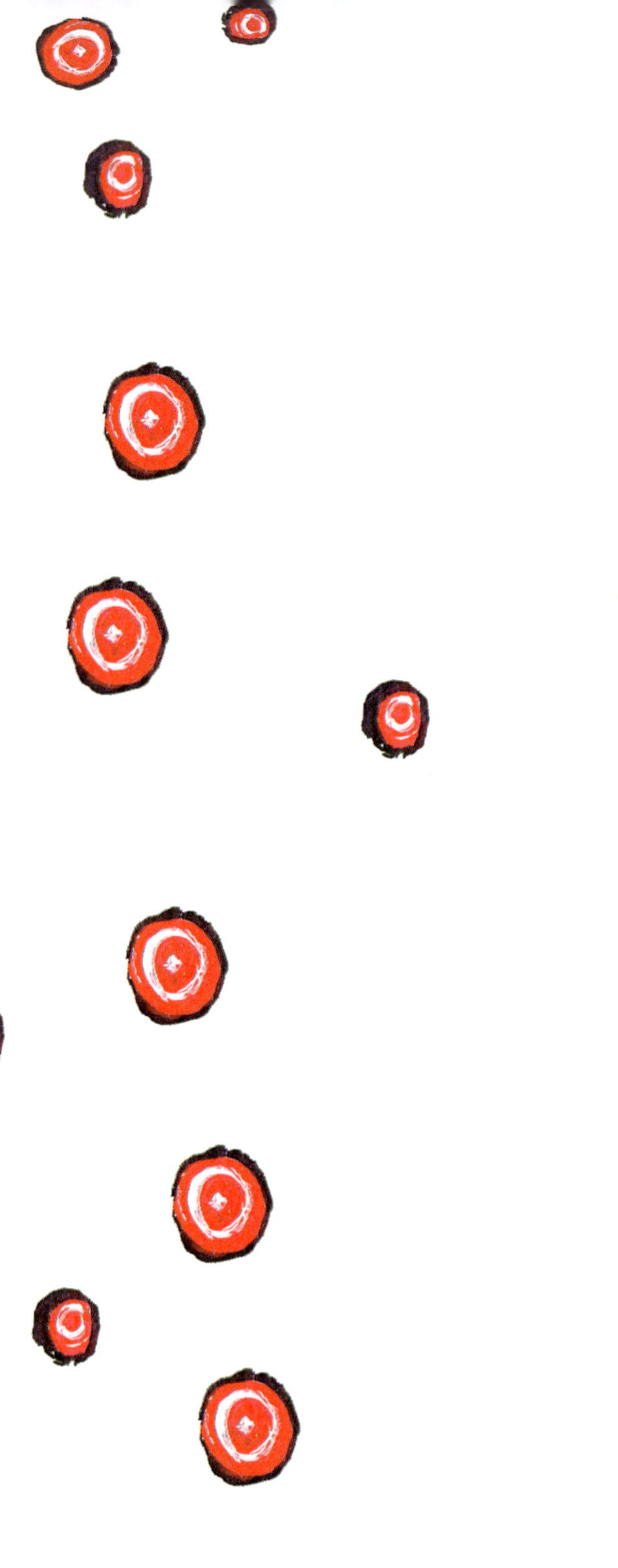

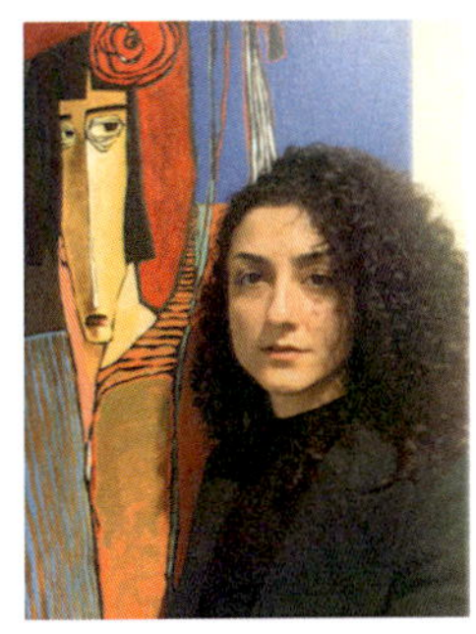

Bahar Taghiani is an illustrator and visual artist whose love for visual imagery began in early childhood. She started by creating characters out of pieces of paper, placing them in imagined stories, and bringing them to life. Today, her artworks are primarily created using mediums such as acrylic, collage, colored pencil, and watercolor, drawing inspiration from her perception of the world around her. Bahar is an award-winning artist, recognized by UNICEF for her illustration in the competition "Children on the Eve of New Year."

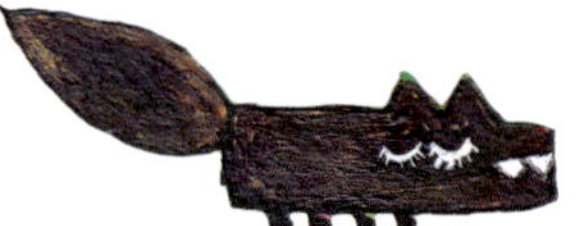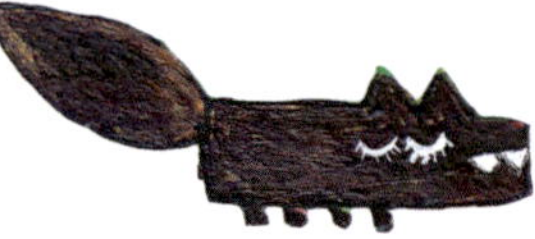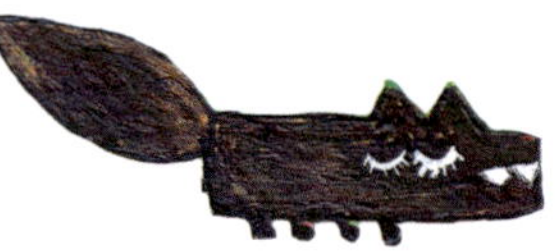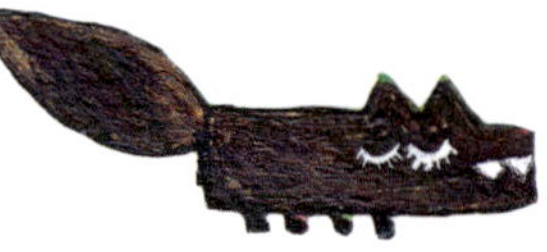

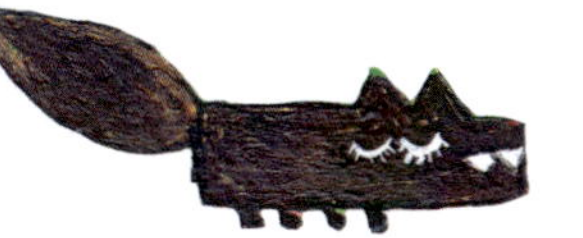
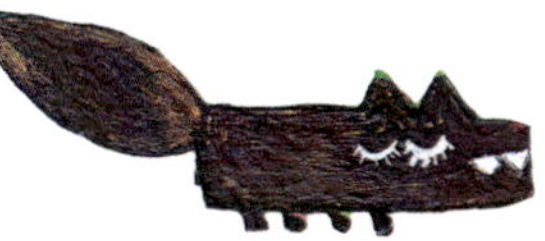
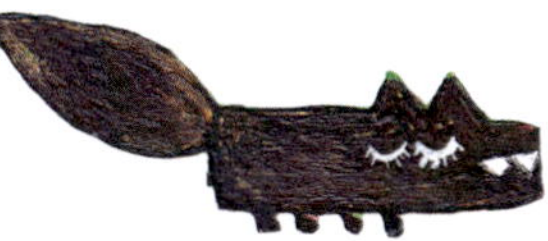
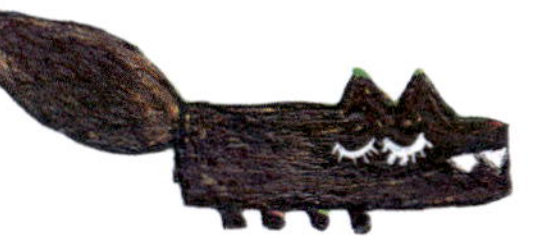

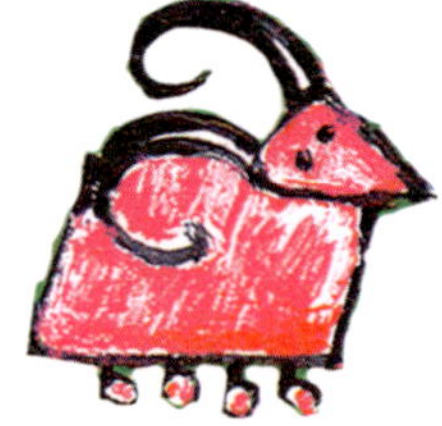

www.ingramcontent.com/pod-product-compliance
Lightning Source LLC
Chambersburg PA
CBRC102023050726
47602CB00013B/168